# Anointing
## *for*
# Possibilities

Andrew V. Pusey

# Anointing for Possibilities

## Published by Cornerstone Publishing

A Division of Cornerstone Creativity Group LLC
Info@thecornerstonepublishers.com
www.thecornerstonepublishers.com

## Author's Contact

To book the author to speak at your next event or to order bulk copies of this book, please, use the information below:

andrewpusey711@yahoo.com

Printed in the United States of America.

# DEDICATION

To my wife, **Odetta Alves-Pusey,** a Proverbs 31
woman with a keen insight into ethics and etiquette.
You often demonstrate wisdom, dignity, and
excellence in all things. You are loyal and continue
to stand by my side through thick and thin; I am
pleased and grateful to you for that; with utmost love,
appreciation and sincerity.

"For with God nothing will be impossible."

Luke 1:37 (NKJV)

# CONTENTS

# ACKNOWLEDGMENTS

In my book, *Anointing for Possibilities*, I couldn't have harnessed so much drive to write this book, had it not been for the help of the Holy Spirit and the various help in my formative years.

I want to acknowledge my wife Odetta, my parents, my family, my friends, my church family, and the Christian community for being kind to me.

Especially, I delightfully acknowledge my Pastor, the late Dr. JA. Douglas, and his wife, Rev. Roslyn Douglas, who were my spiritual parents in the gospel. I want to thank Dr. Michael Hunter for his word of prophecy directed to me concerning the writing of this book.

I am indeed grateful for my community of believers who are a stronghold of faith through these precious moments of advancement in God's kingdom. The kingdom of God is about augmenting in the unleashing of a greater anointing because there is nothing impossible with God.

# INTRODUCTION:

# THE UNLIMITED POSSIBILITIES IN THE ANOINTING

The anointing of the Holy Spirit offers boundless potential. Without it, the believer's journey lacks divine distinction, radiant glory, and vibrant life colors. Yet with it, the door opens to infinite spiritual possibilities. The anointing is a potent force that can radically transform our lives, enabling the believer to perform deeds achievable only through supernatural means.

"The Spirit of the Sovereign Lord is upon me because the Lord has anointed me to bring good news to the humble; he has sent me to bind up the wounded hearts, to proclaim freedom to the captives, and release from darkness to the prisoners; To proclaim the year of the Lord's favor and the day of vengeance of our God; to comfort all who mourn; To bestow upon those who mourn in Zion, to give them a crown of beauty instead of ashes, the oil of joy instead of mourning, and a garment of praise instead of a spirit of despair..." Isaiah 61:1-3

The anointing is God's mighty power at work within and through the believer, enabling him for a potent life and effective ministry. It is a divine gift that empowers us to journey in His power, accomplish our divine calling, and experience the fullness of His presence and blessings in our lives and ministries. It is the tangible manifestation of God's power, made available to and through the believer by the person and work of the Holy Spirit.

Through the anointing, the Holy Spirit works powerfully in and through us to impact others' lives. When we journey in the anointing, we can extend words of wisdom and encouragement, operate with prophetic insight into our lives and the lives of others, and express God's love and compassion in tangible ways. The anointing empowers us to shatter satanic chains, alleviate burdens, heal bodies and hearts, operate in the miraculous, and fulfil the promise Jesus made to His disciples of accomplishing even greater works, leading to transformation and growth in their lives.

The purpose of "Anointing for Possibilities" is to highlight the vast potential of what the anointing of the Holy Spirit can achieve in and through believers. This is not a theological discourse on the anointing but a spiritual classic on its power. In this inspiring journey, we will explore the limitless potential of the anointing, its foundational principles, its various dimensions, and how to nurture and release it through a lifestyle of spiritual hunger, prayer, worship, engagement with the Word, and a heart sensitive to the Holy Spirit. When we journey in the anointing, God can work powerfully through us.

As you delve into these pages, keep an open mind. The insights shared in this book aim to reveal the inherent resources of the anointing and demonstrate how to harness it for divine exploits in your life and ministry. I hope you will be divinely empowered to perform mighty works to the glory of God. Brace yourself to witness the incredible power of the anointing and its transformative influence on your life and ministry.

# 1

## UNDERSTANDING THE ANOINTING

# CHAPTER ONE

# UNDERSTANDING THE ANOINTING

Understanding the anointing is the first and most vital step in leveraging its capacity to generate exploits in life and ministry. Everything in life begins with understanding. In the Kingdom of God, nothing is yours until you understand it. It does not matter whether you have something at your disposal; you need an adequate understanding to enjoy its full benefits. The level to which you can enjoy anything depends on your understanding. In other words, the capacity of anything you have is limited to your understanding of it. You may have in your possession a very sophisticated iPhone, but if you are ignorant of its capabilities, you can only do so much with it. And for many people, all they do is call and receive calls. However, when you decide to study the manufacturer's manual to see what your gadget is capable of doing, you will find out that your I-phone can do much more than the use you currently put it to.

Understanding is the scripturally accredited route to access the benefits that arise from any spiritual reality. For example, when Apostle Paul was to speak to the New Testament church on spiritual gifts, he first addressed the issue of knowledge.

> *"Now, concerning spiritual gifts, brethren, I would not have you ignorant."* 1 Corinthians 12:1

Paul emphasizes that the first step to accessing spiritual gifts and enjoying their full benefits is through knowledge. If you know better, you will do better. Although spiritual gifts were available to them, they needed to gain knowledge and understanding of what spiritual gifts were and how they functioned through the believers to take full advantage of them. It is the same way with the anointing. You can only take advantage of all the possibilities available in and through the anointing when you understand it fully.

That was also why apostle Paul prayed passionately for the young converts (believers) of his day. He prayed that God might enlighten their understanding of who they are, what they have, and what they can do in Christ.

2

*"Wherefore I also, after I heard of your faith in the Lord Jesus, and love unto all the saints, Cease not to give thanks for you, making mention of you in my prayers; That the God of our Lord Jesus Christ, the Father of glory, may give unto you the Spirit of wisdom and revelation in the knowledge of him: The eyes of your understanding being enlightened; that ye may know what the hope of his calling is, and what the riches of the glory of his inheritance in the saints, And what is the exceeding greatness of his power to us-ward who believe, according to the working of his mighty power, Which he wrought in Christ when he raised him from the dead and set him at his right hand in the heavenly places..." Ephesians 1:15-20*

Therefore, the possession and realization of every spiritual reality begin with a thorough understanding of its nature and operation. Understanding is what makes spiritual realities come to life. Once you gain access to light (revelation) about a spiritual reality or a new dimension in God, it is quickened into manifestation. That is why a deep understanding of the anointing is critical. In this chapter, we will explore the anointing and how it works. We will look at examples from the Bible of individuals who were anointed by God and the impact that the anointing had on their lives. We will also examine how the anointing is connected to the Holy Spirit.

## THE CREATIVE POWER OF GOD

Amazingly, He is the first person to be revealed in the scriptures as the creative dimension of God the Father. He was responsible for taking the earth from chaos to beauty. In the first chapter of Genesis, where God carried out what we could, more or less, call a re-creation exercise. The Holy Spirit was the first to be introduced to us.

The First sentence of the entire Bible tells us that God created the Heaven and the Earth. The next thing we read is that the earth was without form and void, and darkness was upon the face of the deep. And the third sentence tells us that the Spirit of God moved upon the face of the waters. So, we know that somewhere in the dimensions of the past, whether millions, billions, or even trillions of years ago, God created the heavens and the earth. We also know that He created it perfectly. When God creates something, it must be good. At least go by the very first verse of chapter one (Genesis 1:1): "In the beginning, God created the heaven and the earth."

It is, therefore, certain that God did not create the earth to be "formless and void." However, the state of chaos which we see there may have been due to Satan's fall. An entire story is left untold and little information is given to explain how this created universe (in Genesis 1:1) became without form and void. From further study, you will find that a part of God's creation involved angels,

4

including Lucifer, who was given custody of certain earthly territory. However, this "super" angel was lifted in his pride, resulting in his fall (Isaiah 14:12-15). And when he fell, he drew approximately one-third of the angels with him. It was this incidence that caused the great chaos that we read about in Genesis 1:2:

> *"And the earth was without form and void, and darkness was upon the face of the deep..." Genesis 1:2*

But God had a better plan for eternity. In this plan, the Power of the Holy Spirit was involved in the creative process. We are told that the Holy Spirit moved before God released the word of command that caused creation to leap into being:

> *"...And the Spirit of God moved upon the face of the waters. And God said, Let there be Light: and there was light." Genesis 1:2*

The Holy Spirit moved upon the face of this chaotic world to put into effect the creative Word of God. He carried out the organizing process, assembling, structuring, and intricately balancing all the elements that composed the ocean. He was responsible for the processes, systems, and structures by which the entire universe runs. Through the work of the Holy Spirit, continents and mountains began to appear as the ocean sought their proper places. He was the power behind the movement of the waters. You would recall that God spoke to the waters and went to gather together in one place, both in heaven and on earth. He structured the waters and the lands. That is the power of the Holy Spirit at work.

The Holy Spirit is the custodian of God's power. That is why He is often referred to as the power of God. He is the Spirit of power.

> *"But ye shall receive power; after that, the Holy Spirit is come upon you." Acts 1:8*

Whenever you witness instances of God's power, whether through healing, deliverance, breakthroughs, or any miraculous events, understand that these are the works of the Holy Spirit. The Holy Spirit embodies the power of God. Just as the invisible force drives the wind, the Holy Spirit is the unseen strength behind the anointing.

## ANOINTING IS SPIRITUAL POWER

The anointing is a holy consecration and an empowerment of the Holy Spirit. The word "anointing" first appears in scripture in the 25th chapter of Exodus. God gave Moses specific instructions about the pattern of the articles of worship and what the people of Israel should present as an offering to Him. It was mentioned concerning the oil (anointing oil).

> *"Oil for the light, spices for anointing oil, and for sweet incense." Exodus 25:6*

In the Old Testament, anointing was used concerning the oil as a symbol of the Spirit of God. In the New Testament, the anointing is associated with the Holy Spirit, who empowers us to live a pleasing life pleasing to God and of extraordinary power and results.

In almost every instance in the Bible, "anointing" refers to pouring oil on someone as a symbol of God's presence and power upon their life. There are other scripturally recognized purposes for using the oil, but the oil is used to consecrate a vessel for holy use. The vessels used in the temples and the priests who ministered in the temple were anointed for holy purposes. It was the anointing that separated them from offering holy services to God. Here are some of the instructions given concerning Aaron and his priestly sons:

> *"Then shalt thou take the anointing oil and pour it upon his head and anoint him. And thou shalt bring his sons and put coats upon them. And thou shalt gird them with girdles, Aaron and his sons, and put the bonnets on them: and the Priest's Office shall be theirs for a perpetual statute: and thou shalt consecrate Aaron and his sons." Exodus 29:7-9*

Although it was the anointing oil that was poured upon them, once it was done as prescribed by God, the Holy Spirit came upon them to separate and empower them for His service. When David was anointed King with the oil, the scriptural says that the Spirit of God came upon him from that day forward.

> *"And the Lord said, Arise, anoint him: for this is he. Then Samuel took the horn of oil and anointed him in the midst of his brethren: and the Spirit of the Lord came upon David from that day forward." 1 Samuel 16:12-13*

So, the oil only symbolizes the Holy Spirit, who comes open to those consecrated for His service. Apart from being consecrated, the anointing supernaturally empowers those who are anointed to do the work designated by God. It would help if you had the anointing to fulfill your purpose and assignment in life.

The anointing is the power of the Holy Spirit at work in the lives of believers. It is not just a force or energy that can be manipulated, but rather a person who can be trusted. The anointing is not about us but God and His power at work in us. When we are filled with the Holy Spirit and operating in the anointing, we have the power of Christ working in us, enabling us to do all things.

The anointing is the yoke destroying, the burden removing the power of God. Whatever is possible with God is possible with his power. If you have someone around you suffering under any form of satanic yoke or burden, you can liberate them by the anointing. We will discuss this in detail in the next chapter.

8

## AS REAL AS ELECTRICITY

The power of the Holy Spirit is just as real as electricity. If you can understand electrify, you can understand the anointing. Put your finger in a live socket, and you will feel the electricity. You will not need to be told you touched power; you will feel the impact. And depending on the level of voltage, you can be knocked down, knocked out, or even electrocuted. If you make contact with a spiritual voltage high enough, it will not only knock you down; it will knock you out. And it will knock out every sickness and disease in your body. It will rid your body of all activities of darkness. That was what happened when that hemorrhaging Woman made her way through the crowd to touch the anointing flowing through Jesus's garment.

She was healed. Hallelujah!

> *"When she had heard of Jesus, she came in the press behind and touched his garment. For she said, If I may touch but his clothes, I shall be whole. And straightway the fountain of her blood was dried up, and she felt in her body that she was healed of that plague." Mark 5:27-29*

You need to make contact with someone who carries the anointing, and you will experience its impact: When you put your hand in the Hand of Jesus, you will feel heaven's power. Yes, you will; it is as real and powerful as electricity. When God's power touches people, they

9

sometimes feel and shake under it. But it is more than the shaking; it is the flow of divine electricity.

## PURPOSE OF THE ANOINTING

In the book Isaiah, the purpose of the anointing was clearly outlined. There is hardly any other passage in scripture that captures as many possibilities of the anointing as the Prophet Isaiah did in his writing. His is a comprehensive outline:

> *"The Spirit of the Lord God is upon me; because the Lord hath anointed me to preach good tidings unto the meek; he hath sent me to bind up the brokenhearted, to proclaim liberty to the captives, and the opening of the prison to them that are bound; To proclaim the acceptable year of the Lord, and the day of vengeance of our God; to comfort all that mourn; To appoint unto them that mourn in Zion, to give unto them beauty for ashes, the oil of joy for mourning, the garment of praise for the spirit of heaviness; that they might be called trees of righteousness, the planting of the Lord, that he might be glorified." Isaiah 61:1-3*

Isaiah began with the declaration, *"The Spirit of the Lord God is upon me because the Lord has anointed me..."* Then he described the purpose of the anointing: to bring good news to the poor, bind up the brokenhearted, proclaim freedom to the captives, release prisoners from darkness, etc.

Later on, in the fourth chapter of the book of Luke, Jesus declared He fulfilled Isaiah's prophecy (Luke 4:18-19. He echoed the very words of the Prophet Isaiah (Isaiah 61:1-3). Jesus declared that he was anointed to preach the Gospel to the poor, heal the brokenhearted, set free captive people, and so on. That statement was not just a powerful declaration of the anointing in action. Still, it was a clear testament to the awesome possibilities available via this life-transforming power of God's Spirit.

The anointing symbolizes the Holy Spirit's power in our lives, enabling us to fulfill our God-given purpose. In other words, the main purpose of the anointing in our lives is empowerment for effective services to God and humanity. The anointing empowers us to do what we cannot do on our own and makes us effective in our service to God. However, it is important to emphasize that the anointing is not reserved for pastors or preachers alone but is available to all who believe in Christ and are willing to deploy it in God's service.

## TWO TYPES OF ANOINTING

There are two types of anointing; based on the working of the Holy Spirit and the believer. Firstly, we have the anointing within. That is the anointing that dwells in you, producing in you a new nature. This corresponds with the work of the Holy Spirit at salvation. The anointing within is the anointing as well. The well of living was a metaphor used by Jesus himself to describe the first

11

operation of the Holy Spirit INSIDE the believer.

*"Jesus answered and said unto her, Whosoever drinketh of this water shall thirst again: But whosoever drinketh of the water that I shall give him shall never thirst; but the water that I shall give him shall be in him a well of water springing up into everlasting life." John 4:13-14*

Notice, it says this water shall be a "well" in him, springing up unto everlasting (or more accurately, eternal life). In other words, that is the anointing you received at the new birth. That's the first time the Holy Spirit entered your life. And just like a well, this anointing is mainly for personal use. Apart from being instrumental to your salvation, this anointing leads and guides you through the affairs of life. It spells out the path you must follow, including understanding the scriptures.

Then, there is the second anointing called the Anointing UPON, which we can be described as the anointing you dwell in. It refers to the second operation of the Holy Spirit in the believer, which happens at the instance of Holy Spirit baptism. At Holy Spirit baptism, the Holy Spirit comes upon you to introduce you to another dimension of operation with God. The metaphor Jesus used here is "a river of living water..."

*"He that believeth on me, as the scripture hath said, out of his belly shall flow rivers of living water. (But this spake he of the Spirit, which they that believe on him should receive: for the Holy Spirit was not yet given;*

*because that Jesus was not yet glorified.) John 7:38-39.*

This can well be called anointing as a river. And just like any river, it has enough water for more than the carrier. A river can cater to a whole community or even much more. And what this portends is that the anointing is for the service of others.

Although these two anointings result from the same source (The Holy Spirit), they differ largely in their function for the believer. When you receive the life of God into your being, the Holy Spirit comes into you to recreate your human Spirit, making you one with God. However, when you are baptized in the Holy Spirit, you are fully immersed in the Holy Spirit as a means to empower you for the work of God. That was why the early disciples of Jesus were asked to wait in Jerusalem until they were supernaturally empowered to do God's work. When this anointing comes upon a believer, he is empowered to operate in the supernatural power of God. And with this power, you can prosecute God's divine assignment effectively.

The people of old could not have the anointing within because they had not yet received the divine nature, which is only possible in Christ, but they had the anointing upon them. When God wanted to use them, he put this anointing on them, although it was not permanent. However, only three groups of people could be anointed: The priests, the prophets, and the Kings. It is empowerment given to them to enable them to fulfill the mandate of their respective offices. This is why David enjoyed this anointing. David was a king, a priest, and a prophet. As a result, he had access to the anointing, and with it, he ruled and governed effectively. He was the shepherd of Israel.

## THE ANOINTING IS IN LEVELS

There is the individual anointing that every believer possesses. There is also a special anointing on the ministry gifts who labor to build the church of God. And then, there is the corporate anointing, which resides in the body of Christ to enable her to carry out God's mandate on earth. This cannot come from a single individual but from a church family. More so, there are levels of anointing. If you read Ezekiel 47, you will see the different levels of the Anointing through Ezekiel's experience in the river. There is the ankle-deep level, the knee-deep level, the waist-deep level, and the overflow level (Ezekiel 47:1-5).

The key lesson here is that anointing is in levels. And so, what is not possible at a low level is possible with a higher level of the anointing. You may use a 3 Kva generator to power a simple home, but you can't use it to power a huge facility with all the equipment and air-conditioning system. That is how it is with the anointing. The level you carry on you determines what you can handle and the problems you can solve. And like electricity, anointing can be generated, stored, or transmitted from one person to another and from humans to material. The anointing is transferable, and the anointing is awesome!

Although we have discussed many things intending to help you understand the anointing, what we have discussed differs from all there is to the anointing. In other words, there is more to the anointing than in this chapter. But I can assure you, if you can truly understand what we have discussed about the anointing, you will be on your way to accessing and enjoying its possibilities.

The anointing is not just a religious concept but a real and tangible force that can change lives beyond our wildest imagination. As we seek the anointing and allow it to work in our lives, we will position ourselves to experience God's power and presence and become more effective vessels for His Kingdom.

# 2

## POWER TO BREAK EVERY YOKE

# CHAPTER TWO

# POWER TO BREAK EVERY YOKE

In a world plagued by various forms of oppression, bondage, and spiritual darkness, the anointing remains an ever-potent force that provides total liberation to humanity. The anointing bestowed upon believers can break every yoke and dismantle the works of darkness. An encounter with the Anointing of the Holy Spirit is an encounter with liberty. The anointing is the divine instrument for liberating humanity from the chains and bondages of the enemy. It was the Prophet Isaiah who declared that the anointing breaks the yoke.

*"And it shall come to pass in that day, that his burden*

> *shall be taken away from off thy shoulder, and his*
> *yoke from off thy neck, and the yoke shall be destroyed*
> *because of the anointing." Isaiah 10:27*

The scripture above is directly talking about the yoke of the Assyrians. At that point in history, the Assyrians opposed Israel on all sides. And the reason is simply that the children of Israel had abandoned God for other gods. They went into idolatry. And just like you see all over the Old Testament, every time the people of God go into idolatry, abandoning the living God; the consequence is that an enemy is allowed to oppress them. A good example is found in the book of Judges. In that particular incident, the children of Israel went into idolatry, resulting in God giving them over to the Midianites who oppressed them.

> *"And the children of Israel did evil in the sight of*
> *the Lord: and the Lord delivered them into the Hand*
> *of Midian seven years. And the Hand of Midian*
> *prevailed against Israel: and because of the Midianites,*
> *the children of Israel made them the dens which are*
> *in the mountains, and caves, and strongholds. And*
> *so it was, when Israel had sown, that the Midianites*
> *came up, and the Amalekites, and the children of the*
> *east, even they came up against them. They encamped*
> *against them, and destroyed the increase of the earth,*
> *till thou come unto Gaza, and left no sustenance for*
> *Israel, neither sheep, nor ox, nor ass. For they came*
> *up with their cattle and their tents, and they came as*

*grasshoppers for multitude; for both they and their camels were without number: and they entered into the land to destroy it. And Israel was greatly impoverished because of the Midianites and the children of Israel cried unto the Lord." Judges 6:1-6*

The children of Israel were oppressed because they left God (Light) for satan (darkness). The logic is quite simple; when another god is invited in, the true God walks out; and when God walks out, the devil (evil) comes in; bringing with it all kinds of bondages, oppression, and activities of darkness. That is why the Bible warns us not to give place to the devil.

This is so important because the devil is an evil opportunist. If you let him into your life and space, he comes in to wreak havoc. The job of the oppressor is to oppress. And so, the devil is not coming into your space to entertain you. Instead, he is coming to fulfill his full mandate to steal, kill and destroy, with you as his object (John 10:10). It is a grave error to let him into your life, family, or business. Of course, the devil does not have the right to oppress a child of God, but when you harbor sin or walk in ignorance, you create an inroad for him. It is this inroad due to sin, disobedience, and ignorance that brings a believer under satanic oppression, bondage, and activities of darkness.

But like the children of Israel, when you repent and submit to the word of God, then your deliverance is guaranteed. Whenever the children of Israel realized their sins and repented, God forgave them and delivered them from their oppressors.

On that basis, the Prophet Isaiah prophesied to the Israelites about God's intention to deliver them from the oppression of the Assyrians via the instrumentality of the anointing. Although Isaiah 10:27 prophecy was directly meant for the nation of Israel at that time, it applies to us as God's children today. Living a life that displeases God can open the door to the devil. But with repentance comes an opportunity for liberty, and just like God promised to destroy the yoke and lift the burdens for Israel back then, He has promised to break every yoke and destroy every burden that the devil may put on God's children today. Truly, the anointing breaks the yoke of darkness and removes every burden in our lives.

The anointing is the burden-removing, yoke-destroying power of the Almighty God. You cannot put a yoke on someone who is truly anointed. If you put a yoke on him, the yoke will break because of the presence of the anointing. And as we saw in chapter one, this power flows from the Holy Spirit, breaking every satanic yoke on humanity.

## A SATANIC YOKE

A yoke is a metaphor for restriction, oppression, and limitation (Isaiah 10:27). Yokes represent the forces that bind and restrict us, preventing us from experiencing true freedom and fulfillment. Yokes also refers to invisible shackles that bind us to behavior patterns, negative mindsets, and destructive cycles.

These yokes manifest in various forms. They can be physical, such as addictions (addiction to sex, drugs, and other undesirable substances that people are addicted to), unhealthy relationships, destructive habits, the yoke of sicknesses, poverty, barrenness, delay stagnation, etc. Emotions, such as fear, anxiety, or past traumas, hinder our emotional well-being. Yokes can also be spiritual, comprising lies, deceptions, and strongholds that keep us in bondage and prevent us from walking in the fullness of our destiny in God. The good news is that regardless of the nature of the yoke you may be grappling with, the Anointing of the Holy Spirit can break it and liberate you from every satanic shackle.

The terrible thing about yokes is that they limit our potential, hinder our progress, and keep us from living the abundant lives we were meant to lead (John 10:10). We must all seek to see how the anointing breaks the yokes of darkness. The truth is, behind every yoke and burden that people live under are demons and demonic activities. In other words, most yokes are demonic. Of course, yokes result from environmental and family factors and other factors; but even many of such yokes have some form of spiritual undertone.

Understanding the forces behind yokes is an important step to dealing with them. Satan understands that the believer's liberty empowers him to fulfill destiny unhindered. He intends to impose all forms of yokes on people, limiting their progress and destiny. He seeks to alter our thinking through deception, lies, and manipulations to separate us from the truth of God's word. Therefore, recognizing his evil schemes becomes invaluable, especially if we intend to break free from all of Satan's yokes. In other words, our choices and actions play a significant role in keeping us under satanic yokes. By our choices and actions, we partner with the devil in bringing these yokes on ourselves. The devil does not operate completely independently of our efforts. Through negative and unscriptural thoughts, words, and actions, we allow him the leverage he has on us.

When you willingly engage in behaviors or patterns that lead to bondage or yokes, you unwittingly create a satanic inroad for his yokes to take over your life. The amazing thing is that such satanic yokes carry very gruesome long-term consequences.

Ultimately, breaking free and staying free from yokes require personal responsibility. Understanding the role of personal responsibility empowers us to make intentional choices that align with God's truths, capable of liberating us from self-destructive habits and patterns.

However, we can always take solace in the fact that the anointing can destroy every form of the yoke, whether spiritual, mental, or physical. As we tap into the transformative power in the anointing, every yoke is destroyed, and every evil burden is supernaturally removed. As a result, we experience liberty—on every side. Since these yokes are the works of darkness, the anointing destroys them through the Light of God. The anointing can introduce Light into the darkest corners of our lives, thereby exposing and destroying all the works of darkness.

## GET HER LOOSED!

This story is in Saint Luke's Gospel of a woman Jesus miraculously healed. This Woman had been disabled for eighteen long years. She was bent over and unable to straighten herself. As a result, she had been burdened by her physical condition, which had caused her great suffering and limited her movement. Her condition can be seen as a yoke, as it bound her and prevented her from living a normal life. And just as the Bible speaks of the "chains of darkness" or the "works of darkness," she was under the oppressive yoke of the devil.

> *"And, behold, there was a woman which had a spirit of infirmity eighteen years, and was bowed together, and could in no wise lift up herself. And when Jesus saw her, he called her to him and said unto her, Woman, thou art loosed from thine infirmity. And he laid his hands on her: and immediately she was made straight, and glorified God." Luke 13:11-13*

25

When Jesus saw her and knew how long she had been under the bondage of Satan, he was eager to break Satan's yoke and liberate her. And that was exactly what He did. He called her to Him and said, "Woman, you are loosed from your infirmity."

With those powerful words, Jesus laid His hands on her. Immediately, a miraculous transformation took place. The Woman felt a surge of divine energy coursing through her body. Her back straightened, and the pain that had plagued her for many years suddenly disappeared. She was completely healed! Filled with joy and gratitude, the Woman praised God. She stood tall and began glorifying the name of the Lord. The people around her were amazed and marveled at the wonderful work that had taken place before their eyes.

Of course, the ruler of the synagogue, true to his religious mentality, reacted in objection and utter hypocrisy. He was upset because Jesus healed her on the sabbath day. On the contrary, Jesus argued that as a seed of Abraham, she deserved to be free.

*"And the ruler of the synagogue answered with indignation because that Jesus had healed on the sabbath day, and said unto the people, there are six days in which men ought to work: in them therefore come and be healed, and not on the sabbath day. The Lord then answered him and said, Thou hypocrite, doth not each one of you on the sabbath lose his ox or his ass from the stall, and lead him away to watering? And ought*

*not this Woman, being a daughter of Abraham, whom Satan hath bound, lo, these eighteen years, be loosed from this bond on the sabbath day?" Luke 13:14-16*

## WHY DO WE NEED THE ANOINTING?

Like that precious Woman, many believers today labor under the burden of the manipulation and bondage of darkness. And until we contend for the Anointing of the Holy Spirit, we cannot enforce their liberty. You must realize that the devil is an evil brute who does not let go except by power. The only language the devil understands is the language of power. He will not listen to your tears or your feeling of frustration; he will ONLY listen to power—a power greater than what he wields.

In other words, when you introduce the Anointing of the Holy Spirit, he has no option but to leave. But only by talking will you recycle your pain and frustration for a long time. This is not a doomsday prophecy; it is just how it works. If you want to eliminate the activities of darkness in your affairs, you must introduce the power of the Holy Spirit. That is why Jesus never sent His disciples without power. When He sent out a seventh of His disciples to preach, he gave them power against the enemy to break his yokes off people's lives.

Another thing about the devil is that he never lets his

prisoners go free. To be free, it must do it by force and by power! Because the devil is the oppressor, force is needed to free the prisoners.

## 1. Jesus came for this.

The beautiful thing is that it is for this reason that Jesus manifested on the earth. He came to eradicate the works of darkness.

> *"For this purpose, the Son of God was manifested, that he might destroy the works of the devil." 1 John 3:8*

Amazingly, not only did He have the noble intention to destroy satan's work, He had the power to force so. The anointing supernaturally empowered Jesus to undo all the deeds of darkness.

> *"The Spirit of the Lord is upon me because he hath anointed me to preach the gospel to the poor; he hath sent me to heal the brokenhearted, to preach deliverance to the captives, and recovering of sight to the blind, to set at liberty them that are bruised." Luke 4:18*

> *"How God anointed Jesus of Nazareth with the Holy Spirit and with power: who went about doing good, and healing all that were oppressed of the devil; for God was with him." Acts 10:38*

Through the Anointing of the Holy Spirit, he can do all the wonderful things recorded in scripture and manifest in our day. And just as the next verse (verse 39) says, we witness it in our day. Everywhere he went, he liberated men from all the works of darkness. He lived true to that assignment. The sick were healed, the blind saw, the lame walked, and the oppressed were set free by the power of God.

## 2. Men and women experienced liberty.

Throughout the Bible, there are numerous examples of individuals and groups of people who experienced the breaking of yokes and the liberation from bondage. For instance, Moses led the Israelites out of slavery in Egypt, Daniel was delivered from the lion's den, and Paul and Silas were freed from prison by an earthquake (Acts 16:25-26). In the New Testament, we also see several liberated people from various forms of bondage. A good example was the Woman who suffered under the yoke of sickness for 12 years. Her condition was gruesome, and she had spent all she had sought a medical cure to no avail. But when she finally realized the power of the anointing, she came in the press and touched Jesus's garment. Instantly, she was healed (Mark 5:28-30). All these examples (and others) highlight the power of God to intervene and set people free from various forms of oppression via anointing.

## STEPS FOR BREAKING YOKES

Here are a few keys strategies to facilitate the process of liberation:

### 1. Identifying the Yokes

The first step in dealing with any oppressive yoke is to identify it. You can call this diagnosis. Diagnosis always comes before the cure. Only when you can identify the yoke in question will you be able to deal with it? Solving a problem you know little or nothing about is challenging.

When yokes are deeply rooted in your life, it could sometimes be difficult to identify. Sometimes, these yokes may come from negative childhood experiences, environmental influences and spiritual forces. Identifying the specific yokes holding you down requires deep understanding, self-introspection and high-level discernment. You can also decipher what yoke to deal with by looking out for its impact on your life or the life of the individual involved. By understanding the root cause of these yokes, we can develop the right strategies to overcome them.

### 2. Renew the Mind

Dealing with the yoke requires intentional mind renewal. When you have been through certain challenging experiences in life, they leave you with a particular mindset, which in most cases, is negative. Changing these negative mindsets will, therefore, require you to renew your mind with God's word. Here is Paul's passionate call to the believers to renew their minds:

> *"And be not conformed to this world: but be ye transformed by the renewing of your mind, that ye may prove what is that good, and acceptable, and perfect, will of God." Romans 12:2*

According to the scripture above, we are transformed by renewing our minds. In Ephesians, Paul speaks about being renewed in the spirit of your mind.

> *"And be renewed in the spirit of your mind." Ephesians 4:23*

When you renew your mind in a particular area of life, you inundate yourself with God's way of thinking, eliminating any yoke associated with that area. Renewing your mind is about challenging negative thought patterns and beliefs that may be reinforcing yokes in your life. As you renew your mind through meditating on the word, you empower your mind with truths that support your journey toward freedom.

## 3. Embrace Scriptural Pattern of Thoughts

The biggest mistake many people make is allowing their mind to drift about independently. They fail to realize that they are solely responsible for their thoughts. As a believer, you must realize that your thoughts are up to you. It's up to you whether you focus on positive and empowering thoughts or negative and disempowering thoughts.

Unfortunately, the world around us constantly bombards us with messages, images, ideas and paradigms that do not align with the Biblical paradigm. The danger is that even well-meaning believers can be caught up in that deadly web, leading to yokes. But the beautiful thing is that we can take control of our thoughts by embracing the template recommended in scripture. In the book of Philippians, Paul reminds us that we must constantly reject those things that do not draw us closer to God and consciously focus on the things that do.

> *"Finally, brethren, whatsoever things are true, whatsoever things are honest, whatsoever things are just, whatsoever things are pure, whatsoever things are lovely, whatsoever things are of good report; if there be any virtue, and if there be any praise, think on these things." Philippians 4:8*

We can only think of pure, lovely, good reports, vitreous and praise-worthy stuff. That implies that we all can choose what we think about. If you want to get your thoughts under control and your life in order, you should align your thoughts with this scriptural template.

The powerful thing about this is that it helps guide your thoughts in the right direction. In other words, any thought that does not meet this scriptural standard does not qualify to occupy your mind at all. As you take control of your thoughts and align yourself with this scriptural template, you will be well on your way to total liberty from every form of the yoke.

# 3

---

## ANOINTED FOR SERVICE

# CHAPTER THREE

# ANOINTED FOR SERVICE

The primary purpose of the anointing is the fulfillment of our God-given assignment. God has called each of us to fulfill a specific purpose in life. Your calling is your God-ordained platform to serve God through serving others. However, not everyone who is called gets to fulfill their calling. It is one thing to be called and a completely different thing to fulfill the calling. To fully manifest your purpose and calling, you need the anointing. I am talking about the same power that enabled the early church apostles to witness powerfully for God.

> *"ye shall receive power, after that the Holy Spirit is come upon you: and ye shall be witnesses unto me both in Jerusalem, and in all Judaea, and in Samaria, and unto the uttermost part of the earth." Acts 1:8*

Unless you carry His power, you can't truly be an effective witness of Christ's resurrection. We can only prove His resurrection by demonstrating His supernatural power in people's lives. This chapter is mainly about the transformative role of the anointing in advancing God's Kingdom and impacting the world. As we explore the connection between the anointing and our calling (service), I hope you will be inspired to seek the anointing and allow it to work in and through you to fulfill God's unique purpose for your life.

## THE ZEAL FOR SERVICE

When the anointing comes upon our calling, it becomes a catalyst for transformation. It ignites a fire within us, a burning passion that fuels our determination to carry out the work assigned to us and births in us the capacity to demonstrate our calling with diverse supernatural manifestations. It takes inner fire to do the work of God, without which your work will be a complete drag.

> *"Not slothful in business; fervent in spirit; serving the Lord." Romans 12:11*

The anointing whispers in our ears guide our steps and unveil hidden truths that quicken us to fulfill our assignments. Sincerely, it is impossible to fulfill your divine assignment without the empowerment of the Holy Spirit. Attempting to do that will only amount to a complete waste of time. This is why Jesus did not allow His disciples to go after their calling without anointing them. He sternly charged His disciples to wait until they received divine empowerment from the Holy Spirit.

> *"And, behold, I send the promise of my Father upon you: but tarry ye in the city of Jerusalem, until ye be endued with power from on high." Luke 24:49*

Jesus knew they needed the anointing to function in their assignment. Even when He was to send them to preach to the Jewish communities, he authorized them—the power to make their work effective. As a result of that power, they discharged their assignment with precision and success and returned with Joy.

> *"And the seventy returned again with joy, saying, Lord, even the devils are subject unto us through thy name." Luke 10:17*

Christians have been mandated to preach the Gospel to every nation worldwide (Mathew 28:18-19). A mandate goes with a clear assignment of what to accomplish, authorization to carry out the mandate, and empowerment. Without the requisite empowerment, the mandate will fail. The Gospel we have been mandated to preach is a gospel of power. Therefore, we need an ever-increasing anointing to do the task of reaching the world with the Gospel. Our God-assigned task must be discharged with the aid of the supernatural. And for that, God seeks to equip us with His manifold power adequately.

As recipients of the anointing, we are called vessels of transformation and agents of change. By releasing the anointing in ministry and service, we bring healing, deliverance, and restoration to others, ushering in God's Kingdom on Earth.

## ANOINTING AND MIRACLES

The anointing is not a passive or dormant force; but a dynamic power that manifests through miracles, signs, and wonders. Miracles are extraordinary events that defy natural laws and human understanding. They are powerful demonstrations of the tangible Anointing of the Holy Spirit at work. The anointing catalyzes miracles as it taps into the divine realm and causes supernatural experiences to manifest on Earth. Miracles can manifest as physical healing, financial breakthroughs, restoration of relationships, or any situation where divine intervention is required.

The Ministry of Miracles, signs, and Wonders is a means to preach the Gospel effectively. It takes a radical demonstration of the power of God to get the job done. Theology will not do it at all. The Bible says that our Gospel is not in word only but in power.

*"For our gospel came not unto you in word only, but also in power, and in the Holy Spirit." 1 Thessalonians 1:5*

When it comes down to it, power is what it takes to get the job done. If we don't carry this powerful message of Pentecost with power, God will raise a people who will. Now is the time for us to spread the Gospel like never before. Through Calvary, we entered God's presence; through Pentecost, God's presence and power entered us, empowering us for a productive ministry.

In Acts of the Apostle, we see how the Gospel gained ground through the ministry of miracles. One of the reasons the people of Samaria opened up their hearts to heed the Gospel preached by Philip was the miracles.

*"Therefore they that were scattered abroad went everywhere preaching the word. Then Philip went down to the city of Samaria and preached Christ unto them. And the people with one accord gave heed unto those things which Philip spake, hearing and seeing the miracles which he did. For unclean spirits, crying with loud voice, came out of many that were possessed with them: and many taken with palsies, and that were lame, were healed." Acts 8:4-7*

This was not only an occurrence with Philip alone but a usual occurrence with all the other apostles of Jesus.

> *"And with great power gave the apostles witness of the resurrection of the Lord Jesus: and great grace was upon them all." Acts 4:33*

And all these were made possible because of the anointing. The Anointing of the Holy Spirit is the secret behind every manifestation in people's lives, whether in Jesus' earthly ministry, the early apostles, or today's Christians. Miracles played a significant role in the success of Jesus' earthly ministry. All through the ministry of Jesus on earth, we are told that a multitude followed. And the reason for that level of followership is the miracles that He did.

> *"When he was come down from the mountain, great multitudes followed him. And, behold, there came a leper and worshipped him, saying, Lord, if thou wilt, thou canst make me clean. And Jesus put forth his hand, and touched him, saying, I will; be thou clean. And immediately his leprosy was cleansed." Matthew 8:1-3*

> *"And a great multitude followed him because they saw his miracles which he did on them that were diseased." John 6:2*

The more people knew about the miracles Jesus did, the more they gathered and followed Him. Amazingly, like Jesus needed the anointing to fulfill his assignment, by serving His generation, we all need the anointing to fulfill ours.

# JESUS, OUR ULTIMATE MODEL

If you are looking for a model of a man who operated in the tangible Anointing of the Holy Spirit, look at Jesus. Jesus is usually referred to as Jesus Christ; or Jesus the Christ. Christ is not the surname name of Jesus like we have Jefferson, in Jack Jefferson; no. Christ (Christos in Greek) means the anointed one and His Anointing. Jesus Christ is anointed, but his anointing flows like a river from him, the Head, down to his earthly body through the Holy Spirit. Jesus is the Head, and we are His earthly Body (The Church). The Holy Spirit is God's Anointing abiding in earthly vessels. For this reason, the Bible talked about treasure in earthen vessels.

> *"But we have this treasure in earthen vessels, that the excellency of the power may be of God, and not of us." 2 Corinthians 4:7*

As God's children, we are a royal priesthood; we have been made Kings and Priests unto God.

Anointing is not a feeling, an idea, or an atmosphere. The anointing is the tangled presence of the almighty God among men. It is the assurance that God is with us. The Old Testament prophesied the coming of the Messiah, and the New Testament faithfully records the fulfillment of those prophecies with the birth and ministry of Christ Jesus. The anointing is a person, Emmanuel, God with us, Messiah, the Christ. Jesus

43

Christ is the fountainhead of all anointing.

He is the root of David and our true Messiah. In chapter one of this book, we did mention that in the Old Testament time, only prophets, priests, and Kings were anointed or consecrated with oil to set them apart unto their Office of authority and leadership. Jesus is The very Anointing of God; he is the Prophet, the Priest, and the King of Kings. The corporate anointing for Kingdom building is the threefold Anointing of the Prophet, Priest, and King that abides upon and within us all. Christ produces the Kingdom, the Prophet produces righteousness, the Priest produces peace, and the King produces Joy.

> *"For the kingdom of God is not meat and drink, but righteousness, and peace, and joy in the Holy Spirit."*
> *Roman 14:17*

That is the corporate anointing available to us as a body. And these are all embodied in Christ. Christians must see Jesus as God's anointed one and our savior. Jesus was anointed to do good. He rendered service to humanity, solved problems, answering questions, and met needs wherever He went.

> *"How God anointed Jesus of Nazareth with the Holy Spirit and with power: who went about doing good, and healing all that were oppressed of the devil; for God was with him." Acts 10:38*

Once you embrace and receive the person of the Holy Spirit through your new birth experience and receive the baptism of the Holy Spirit, you make yourself a candidate for the flow of the power of God. The presence of the Anointing of the Holy Spirit in our lives completely changes everything.

## JUST LIKE ADAM

The Holy Spirit helps us to comprehend the length, breadth, and height of

the Love Christ. He empowers us with the fullness of God (Ephesians 3:19). We receive this through the baptism of the Holy Spirit. The Anointing for Service begins with Holy Spirit baptism. We are empowered with the Holy Spirit at Holy Spirit baptism to enable and position us for effective service (ministry). Jesus sent us the Holy Spirit baptism, so we might have the power to implement these blessings. In other words, He made us the children of power. If we are Children of power, we have access to all the power and blessings of God's storehouse.

This is just like the first Adam originally had. God used to walk and talk with Adam and Eve in the Garden of Eden. Adam had power and dominion; he was clothed with glory and power. Adam had the presence of God and a garment of Light. He had power and dominion because he was in God's image and in close communication. If you want to know the dominion

45

and power of the first Adam, just look at the Second Adam (the Lord Jesus Christ). We are not complete without Jesus Christ's dominion in our lives. If we live in the Spirit, we must walk in the Spirit (Galatians 5:25). Through the Holy Spirit baptism, God made it possible for us to have what Adam had. We can make a significant difference in our world through the Anointing of the Holy Spirit.

## ANOINTING FOR YOUR OFFICE

When Jesus rose from the dead, He gave gifts to men. That is what we refer to as ministry gifts today: Ministry gifts include; the Apostles, Prophets, Evangelists, pastors, and teachers.

> *"But unto every one of us is given grace according to the measure of the gift of Christ. Wherefore he saith, When he ascended up on high, he led captivity captive and gave gifts unto men. (Now that he ascended, what is it but that he also descended first into the lower parts of the earth? He that descended is the same also that ascended up far above all heavens, that he might fill all things.) And he gave some, apostles; and some, prophets; and some, evangelists; and some, pastors and teachers; For the perfecting of the saints, for the work of the ministry, for the edifying of the body of Christ."*
> *Ephesians 4:7-12*

Every one of these ministry gifts is ordained by Jesus and empowered by the Holy Spirit to fulfill their assignment and mandate. In other words, there is an anointing for your Office and assignment. Once you discover your Office, realize and pursue its anointing. An anointing exists for the apostle, Prophet, evangelist, pastor, and teacher. And with each of these gifts comes the requisite anointing to effectively discharge the duties of such an office.

One of the ways you discern your Office and Anointing is to look out for the areas where you operate with maximum ease. If you lack ease in your operation, there is no grace there. And if there is no grace, then chances are you are not called to that Office. And when you find your Office and Anointing, stay there. Master how to operate the anointing in your life. That way, you will jog only to make an impact and become outstanding in journey calling and assignment.

## EQUIPPED WITH SPIRITUAL GIFTS

The anointing enables us to serve effectively by empowering us with spiritual gifts. You are divinely enabled and gifted by the Grace of God to do what he has placed you on earth to do. The anointing equips us with the necessary gifts and abilities to fulfill our calling. He freely distributes these gifts of His own volition. Of course, we are encouraged to covet them; but ultimately, He is the giver.

> *"But the manifestation of the Spirit is given to every man to profit withal. For to one is given by the Spirit*

*the word of wisdom; to another the word of knowledge by the same Spirit; To another faith by the same Spirit; to another the gifts of healing by the same Spirit; To another the working of miracles; to another prophecy; to another discerning of spirits; to another divers kinds of tongues; to another the interpretation of tongues: But all these worketh that one and the selfsame Spirit, dividing to every man severally as he will." 1 Corinthians 12:7-11*

*"But unto every one of us is given grace according to the measure of the gift of Christ." Ephesians 4:7*

*"As every man hath received the gift, even so, minister the same one to another, as good stewards of the manifold grace of God. If any man speaks, let him speak as the oracles of God; if any man minister, let him do it as of the ability which God giveth: that God in all things may be glorified through Jesus Christ, to whom be praise and dominion forever and ever. Amen." 1 Peter 4:10-11*

The Holy Spirit, the source of the anointing, distributes spiritual gifts to believers for the improvement and growth of the church. As we tap into the anointing, we are given the gifts to fulfill our calling and impact the world.

The anointing gives us the power and authority to fulfill our calling. When anointed, we can do things we could not do on our own. We are empowered to overcome obstacles, impact lives, and fulfill the unique purpose that God has for us. That is the reality of the supernatural life only possible by the Holy Spirit. Here are a few other ways the ministry of the Holy Spirit directly impacts our service or ministry.

**1. The Holy Spirit empowers us to Preach like Jesus:**

- The Holy Spirit anointed Jesus to preach.
- Jesus preached the word with power.
- Jesus preached in the synagogues.
- He preached that the Kingdom of heaven is at hand.
- He preached from city to city.
- He did not even preach in one city for too long. He said, "I have other cities to go and preach to as well."

**2. The Holy Spirit gives power for service:**

Consider these questions for a moment:

- How can we fly a jet plane with no fuel?
- How can we fight a war with no guns?
- How can we use electric fans with no electricity?
- How can we run a vehicle with no batteries?
- How can we work out our salvation without the power of the Holy Spirit?

### 3. The Holy Spirit helps us to win souls like Jesus:

- Jesus came into the world to save sinners.
- The Holy Spirit magnifies Jesus.
- Jesus was the master soul winner.
- Jesus won souls whether the crowd was large or small.
- The Holy Spirit makes you a partner with God.
- He reproves the world of sin, righteousness, and Judgement.
- The Holy Spirit helps us to preach with boldness.

## RUSH FOR OPPORTUNITIES

Once empowered, we should actively seek avenues to serve, striving to influence the lives of those around us positively. Expanding God's Kingdom demands an openness to divine opportunities, stepping beyond our comfort zones, attuning ourselves to the Holy Spirit's guidance, and capitalizing on chances to impart the anointing's power to others. We become catalysts for change and influence by being mindful of our needs, responding with empathy and wisdom, and letting the anointing steer our engagements.

Employing our spiritual gifts, talents, and capabilities in ministering and serving is a potent way to deploy the transformative power of the anointing. We can address others' needs, bringing about healing, liberation, and renewal. Whether through preaching, teaching, counseling, or demonstrating kindness and service in various ways, we act as conduits for the anointing, altering lives, and offering hope to those in despair.

As we strive to fulfill our divine calling, the anointing supports us. Although the journey may be filled with hurdles and opposition, the anointing gives us the resilience and stamina to persist and fulfill our spiritual assignments.

It is undeniable that in these times, the body of Christ needs divine power more than ever. Only the extraordinary power of God can counter the wave of sin, illness, wickedness, and perversion inundating our world. Remarkably, the anointing is authentic and cannot be counterfeited; one either possesses it or not.

To truly experience the tangible anointing of the Holy Spirit, we must be prepared to make the necessary sacrifices to activate, nurture, and grow within it. Undertaking God's work without His power is a recipe for failure. But if we strive to access the anointing of the Holy Spirit, we can expect exponential results in our lives and ministries, accompanied by continually expanding glory and impact.

# 4

---

## EXPERIENCING SUPERNATURAL ABUNDANCE

# CHAPTER FOUR

# EXPERIENCING SUPERNATURAL ABUNDANCE

A young missionary ventured to pioneer a church in a small African town. He had little or no possessions to his name and no instruments, partners, or financial support. Consequently, his daily affairs proved to be quite challenging. However, fueled by his firm conviction in his calling, he preached the gospel to the locals.

One thing was certain: he carried a powerful anointing on his life. After surveying the community's needs, he organized a crusade to establish a local church. After sharing his vision with a few locals, he managed to recruit five volunteers whom he trained for the upcoming crusade. On the appointed day, with the assistance of his volunteers, he orchestrated the event and welcomed the attendees.

The crusade was awe-inspiring as the missionary fervently preached under the anointing of the Holy Spirit. The power of God was evident as many locals experienced miraculous healings and deliverances. Notably, three individuals afflicted with leprosy were supernaturally healed.

Remarkably, a wealthy young man who had returned home from the United States of America happened to be present at the crusade. After its conclusion, he approached the missionary, warmly greeting him and expressing gratitude for organizing such an impactful event in his community. Just before departing, he reached into his pocket, retrieved his business card, handed it to the missionary, and said, "Please see me tomorrow morning; I would love to partner with you."

The missionary packed up his belongings with the help of the volunteers and left. The following day, he contacted the young businessman using the provided business card and arranged a meeting.

He left that meeting with cash, more than enough to sustain his ministry for over six months. The businessman pledged to send him an offering each month as if that were insufficient. Moreover, upon his return to the United States, he sent the missionary a complete set of musical equipment. Consequently, the missionary officially employed the volunteers who had worked with him and hired three additional individuals, enabling him to expand the crusade to other communities.

This story imparts several valuable lessons, the most significant being that supernatural provision is real and makes a difference in our life's endeavors.

While we embrace this reality, it is crucial to recognize that advancing the gospel on a large scale requires substantial financial resources.

## THE GOD OF ABUNDANCE

Amazingly, God is ever willing and able to supply all our needs and desires abundantly. Not only that, God is the God of abundance; abundance is a scriptural reality. Supernatural abundance is all about divine intervention and the manifestation of extraordinary blessings in our finances and lives.

God can supply everything we need to lead an abundant life here. He can make supernatural provisions available for His children and their life's assignment. And while we bask in this reality, it's vital to realize that walking in supernatural abundance is never an option for the believer. That is the life we were designed to have. We are saved and called to live a life of abundance:

> *"The thief cometh not, but for to steal, and to kill, and to destroy: I come that they might have life and have it more abundantly." John 10:10*

God wants you to walk in so much abundance it won't be a big deal to fund the gospel. It is through prosperity that God's kingdom can spread abroad. Here is how prophet Zechariah puts it: "Cry yet, saying, thus saith the Lord of hosts; My cities through prosperity shall yet be spread abroad; and the Lord shall yet comfort Zion, and shall yet choose Jerusalem." Zechariah 1:17

## YOU NEED EMPOWERMENT

However, you need supernatural empowerment to prosper and enjoy such supernatural abundance. And that is where the anointing of the Holy Spirit becomes very relevant. As a child of God, you must realize that it takes the anointing to prosper. Of course, there are laws to apply to provoke abundance, but you need empowerment by the Spirit to get the financial results you passionately desire. In the book of Deuteronomy, God promised to empower us for prosperity and wealth.

> *"But thou shalt remember the Lord thy God: for it is he that giveth thee power to get wealth, that he may establish his covenant which he sware unto thy fathers, as it is this day." Deuteronomy 8:18*

God is the one who gives us the power to make wealth. And the purpose of this empowerment for abundance is the establishment of His covenant. God's covenant is represented by the church and its mandate to spread the gospel. Without finance, the gospel will be limited in its reach. Although it is very powerful to transform individuals, families, communities, and nations, it will not see the light of day without resources to drive it.

God blesses us so we can bless the world around us. In other words, God's major motivation for supplying us with abundance is His kingdom. God intends to bless us like Abraham so that the gospel can spread worldwide through us. Evil sometimes seems more attractive and thriving than the gospel (a force for good) because evil has more dedicated funders than righteousness. But I see it changing for good in Jesus' name!

The anointing connects us to the limitless resources of God, enabling us to receive divine provision beyond our human limitations. When we operate under the anointing, we can trust that God will supply all our needs abundantly.

> *"But my God shall supply all your need according to his riches in glory by Christ Jesus." Philippians 4:19*

The anointing is a tangible expression of God's power and favor upon His people. God's power in and on you connects you with the spiritual realm, enabling you to operate in a supernatural dimension. And usually, the result comes in the form of divine favor, provision, and abundance. Through the anointing, God's grace abounds in our lives.

> *"And God is able to make all grace abound toward you, that you, always having all sufficiency in all things, may have an abundance for every good work."*
> *2 Corinthians 9:8*

This grace meets our needs and equips us to fulfill our purpose and bless others abundantly. To fully understand this, we would need to read it in the Amplified version:

> *"And God is able to make all grace (every favor and earthly blessing) come to you in abundance, so that you may always and under all circumstances and whatever the need be self-sufficient [possessing enough to require no aid or support and furnished in abundance for every good work and charitable donation]." 2 Corinthians 9:8*

God wants everything to come to us in a great proportion to enable us to care for ourselves and others. He wants you and me to be self-sufficient, so we won't need anyone's assistance. This is so powerful! And that is the life we are called to live.

# HOW THE ANOINTING BRINGS ABOUT ABUNDANCE

Through the anointing, a person can experience a level of abundance that goes beyond the natural realm. And that is what this chapter is all about- tapping into the supernatural abundance by the anointing; paying attention to God's word is essential. This process involves a combination of spiritual practices, the renewal of your mind, and alignment with God's principles. Through anointing, you can attract not only financial blessings but you will also experience a significant increase in resources. That could come in unexpected opportunities, promotions, business success, or divine provision in times of need. To enjoy such benefits, here are a few principles to unlock supernatural abundance:

## 1. The giving anointing.

To operate in abundance, you must become a giver. Giving is the most basic principle for activating supernatural abundance. According to the scriptures, you can only reap what you sow (Galatians 6:7, Genesis 8:22). Expecting to walk in financial abundance without embracing generosity is a complete waste of time. Every time you talk about supernatural abundance, you must explore the concept of grace and faith. Remember, grace makes the provision, but faith makes the withdrawal— taking practical delivery of all that Jesus' death, burial, resurrection, and ascension made available for us. But when you touch on grace, you have to look at giving.

It takes grace to give. It takes the anointing to part with something valuable to you. Paul called it grace for generosity (2 Corinthians 9); Jesus referred to it as the power to lay it down. "No man taketh it from me, but I lay it down of myself. I have the power to lay it down, and I have the power to take it again." John 10:18

## 2. Anointing for Divine leading.

Our prosperity as God's children is tied to divine leading (Psalm 23:1). This is a solid way the anointing brings about the supernatural provision in our lives. Divine leading is a powerful leg to the realm of abundance. If you can hear God clearly through the anointing of the Holy Spirit, you cannot be poor. The Holy Spirit not only teaches us, but He also leads us and guides us on the path of supernatural provision and abundance.

> *"Thus saith the Lord, thy Redeemer, the Holy One of Israel; I am the Lord thy God which teacheth thee to profit, which leadeth thee by the way that thou shouldest go. O that thou hadst hearkened to my commandments! Then had thy peace been as a river, and thy righteousness as the waves of the sea... And they thirsted not when he led them through the deserts: he caused the waters to flow out of the rock for them: he clave the rock also, and the waters gushed out." Isaiah 48:17-18, 21*

The anointing brings a heightened spiritual discernment and insight, allowing individuals to receive divine guidance. This guidance is crucial in making wise decisions, taking the right steps, and positioning oneself for abundance. Through the anointing, individuals are led into paths of prosperity and blessings. The anointing helps individuals align their lives with the divine will, purpose, and principles. By surrendering to the divine guidance received through the anointing, individuals have been led away from dangerous paths and towards those aligned with abundance. This alignment ensures that individuals operate in harmony with the divine flow of provision.

### 3. Overcoming Obstacles with the Anointing.

One of the key things you must understand about anointing is that it breaks the yoke of bondage and releases us from burdens that hinder our progress. It paves the way for supernatural abundance by removing obstacles on our destiny path.

> *"And it shall come to pass in that day, that his burden shall be taken away from off thy shoulder, and his yoke from off thy neck, and the yoke shall be destroyed because of the anointing." Isaiah 10:27*

> *Trials and challenges are a part of life; we all face them eventually. However, with the anointing, we have the power to overcome these obstacles and emerge victorious.*

### 4. The Multiplication effect.

The anointing has a multiplication effect. Anything it touches multiplies. It multiplies resources, influence, spiritual gifts, kingdom impact, and the expansion of vision and dreams. Some people call it the X-factor. This X-factor brings about exponential growth in various areas of life.

Just as the five loaves and two fishes were multiplied to feed the multitude, the anointing can bring abundance, breakthroughs, and supernatural increase. By operating under the anointing, you can experience a multiplication that far surpasses human understanding and expectations. That is how you know it's the anointing.

Whether it was the oil that flowed from the widow's jar of oil in the time of Elisha (2 Kings 4:1-7), or the miraculous multiplication of loaves and fishes by Jesus (Mark 6:38-44), the anointing unlocks supernatural abundance. Of course, there are several other means by which the anointing could bring about abundance, but I chose to share these few so you can recall and apply them appropriately. I welcome you to your new level of abundance!

# 5

---

# HEALING BODIES
# AND HEARTS

# CHAPTER FIVE

# HEALING BODIES AND HEARTS

The greatest tragedy that has befallen the human race since the world's creation is sin. Through sin, Adam surrendered to Satan's authority and became a slave of sin. And with sin came sickness and death. That is the reason humanity grapples with the burden of sicknesses and diseases.

Today, many people are bedeviled with all kinds of health challenges. For some, their health condition requires only good medical attention. In other words, the right medical treatment will suffice for them to recover. But for many others, it just isn't so. Such people's health condition is way beyond the capacity of medicine. Some have already been presented with a horrible medical prognosis, giving them no chance at life.

Almost everywhere you turn, you find sick people who have lost all hope of regaining their health. Some people have not made any headway despite consulting the best medical experts. Despite all efforts, all hope seems to be lost. Many people have already been abandoned to their fate due to the critical state of their health. Yet amid all these, one could wonder if there is any way out.

Should sick people give up all hope of ever recovering, or is there a way out? Is there any hope in God? Does God have the answer to the vast health challenge we may face today? Is there a healing plan for God's people? Or should they expect to go through the same gruesome health ordeals as unbelievers?

If you are grappling with these concerns or facing any debilitating health challenges, I have good news for you. God has a healing plan for you! He intends to rid your body of every sickness and disease, no matter how difficult it may seem.

The truth is that God's ultimate intention for us as His beloved children is complete wholeness. He yearns to see His children free of sickness and diseases. That is what His words say:

*"Beloved, I wish above all things that thou mayest prosper and be healthy, even as thy soul prospereth."*
3 John 2

Not only does God wants us to prosper in our body, but He also wants us to prosper in our soul. In other words, our physical, mental, emotional, and material well-being is important to God.

God told the Children of Israel, "I will put none of these diseases upon thee, which I have brought upon the Egyptians: for I am the Lord that healeth thee." Exodus 15:26

In other words, divine healing is a scriptural imperative. God promises to heal His people and keep them whole. God did not only keep His promise to heal them; He went ahead to bless them with sound health. During Israel's journey through the wilderness, we are told that none of them fell ill; instead, every one of them remained strong.

*"He brought them forth also with silver and gold: and there was not one feeble person among their tribes."*
Psalm 105:37

There was not one feeble person among their tribe. Can you imagine that? Imagine relocating over 3 million people across countries, including children, babies, and women. Not one person got sick or died along the way (except those who erred against God). "Is that even possible?" You may ask. Oh yes! God made it happen. He ensured that none of them fell ill or died prematurely.

Now, if you are worried about whether God can heal or keep you healthy, worry no more! He is a God that makes and keeps His promises. And He can keep his healing promises to you.

But while we bask in the euphoria that divine healing is God's promise to us, it is crucial to recognize that this healing flows through the Holy Spirit. Remember, the Holy Spirit is the custodian of God's power—the anointing. The anointing can remarkably transform our physical bodies and ensure wholeness in our souls. It is God's ordained conduit through which God's healing power is channeled into our lives. Like a river flowing steadily, the Holy Spirit carries the healing virtues of God, touching every aspect of our being and making us completely whole. We can, therefore, tap into God's power and be healed.

## THE HEALING ANOINTING

When the anointing manifests in this way, bringing about bodily and emotional well-being, it is termed the healing anointing. The healing anointing is a spiritual gift that offers solace, rejuvenation, and restoration to man's total being. God intends that the anointing of the Holy Spirit should bring healing to everyone needing healing. He wants you healed of every sickness and disease the devil puts on you. Of course, our decisions and lifestyles play a significant role in determining our health conditions. Still, regardless of the source of the sickness or disease, we can decide to yield to the anointing and receive our healing.

The healing anointing is an aspect of the anointing responsible for healing. It is simply the flow of God's power into the body of the sick to bring about healing and deliverance to that person. The thing about the anointing is that it flows.

The healing anointing is like a river. River is a metaphor often used for the anointing. In more than two places in scripture, the anointing is represented with the metaphors of water, rain, or river. In the book of John, the anointing was first called a well of water (John 4:14) and later as a river of living water (John 7:37). In the book of Ezekiel, the prophet Ezekiel uses a river as a metaphor to describe the different level of the anointing. It flows to bring about healing to the nations. It started with ankle-deep, knee-deep, waist-deep, and then an uncrossable river.

> *"And when the man that had the line in his hand went forth eastward, he measured a thousand cubits, and he brought me through the waters; the waters were to the ankles." Ezekiel 47:3*

The Holy Spirit is likened to a mighty river, surging with the life-giving waters of healing, ready to overflow and saturate our lives with divine healing and health. The beautiful thing we notice about this particular river is that it brings healing wherever it goes. We are told that every dead thing that makes contact with it comes alive.

> *"Then said he unto me, These waters issue out toward the east country, and go down into the desert, and go into the sea: which being brought forth into the sea, the waters shall be healed. And it shall come to pass, that everything that liveth, which moveth, whithersoever the rivers shall come, shall live: and there shall be a very great multitude of fish because these waters shall come thither: for they shall be healed, and everything shall live whither the river cometh." Ezekiel 47:8-9*

We can also liken the anointing to gentle rain showers which come down to nourish the barren earth causing the seed to sprout (Isaiah 55:12). It is the rain of the anointing that turns desolate lands into fruitful fields, and fruitful fields into a forest blooming with new life. Hallelujah! When the anointing truly falls on your life, it eliminates the negatives and enhances the positives. It's completely amazing!

Another metaphor for the anointing is oil. It is the most used metaphor in describing the anointing. David declared in Psalms, "But my horn shalt thou exalt like the horn of a unicorn: I shall be anointed with fresh oil." Psalm 92:10

In the parable of the ten virgins, Jesus used oil for the lamp to represent the anointing. Those with lamps but no extra oil (or anointing) were disqualified from meeting the bridegroom (Matthew 25:1-12).

Just as oil relieves dry and cracked skin, the anointing soothes and restores our health, riding the bodily of all forms of infirmities. Like a skilled physician, it penetrates deep into our cells, revitalizing them and triggering a flow of divine life in our entire being. It is through the anointing that broken bones are mended, diseased organs are healed, blind eyes are open, deaf ears hear, and bodily strength is renewed. It binds up the brokenhearted, breathing new life into shattered dreams and guiding us toward total healing and well-being.

The anointing is like fire; it burns and consumes everything that is not of God along its path. When the healing anointing encounters sicknesses and diseases, it consumes it like fire would consume a pack of trash. If you operate in the anointing, you will never accept or tolerate sickness another day.

## SICKNESS HAS BEEN DEALT WITH

By sending his son Jesus into the world to deal with sin, God dealt with sickness once and for all. With that once gruesome death of Jesus, God forever satisfied the claim of justice. Just as David used one stone to bring down Goliath, so did God use Jesus' redemptive sacrifice to bring down both sin, sickness, and death. That one stroke gave us eternal salvation and a life of total victory over sickness, diseases, and death.

> *"Christ hath redeemed us from the curse of the law, being made a curse for us: for it is written, Cursed is everyone that hangeth on a tree." Galatians 3:13*

In other words, God's ultimate provision for our healing is found in Christ. Although God has dealt with sickness, we must take steps to appropriate it both in our lives and the lives of many others. And it is through the anointing that this healing flows to the lives of everyone in need. God anointed Jesus to be the solution to all of man's problems.

> *"How God anointed Jesus of Nazareth with the Holy Spirit and with power: who went about doing good, and healing all that were oppressed of the devil; for God was with him." Acts 10:38*

Through the anointing, man can receive healing and deliverance from all oppressions of the devil. It is also by the anointing that we can heal the sick, cast out devils, mend broken hearts and reclaim everything that man lost through the fall of Adam.

## WHO TOUCHED ME?

It was through the healing anointing that the woman with the issue of blood received her healing. This particular woman was hemorrhaging for 12 excruciating years. According to the scripture, she had spent all her livelihood on medical doctors, searching endlessly for medical solutions to her ailment, just like many people do today. But thank God she finally learned about Jesus and how His anointing was healing many others. Her faith was all-built, and she was ready to dare the consequences of stepping out in public without notice. In her day, people with similar conditions were required to carry an "I'm unclean" tag or badge around.

The reason is that you are regarded as unclean if you are hemorrhaging or leprous. And so, if you happen to touch others, you make them unclean as well. Suffering from such an ailment was not only burdensome, it was traumatizing. But despite all that, she came through the press to touch the helm of Jesus' garment.

She understood something about the anointing that only very few people of today understand. She knew that the anointing flows and that she knew that it could flow like current from any material that makes contact with the anointed. And true to her faith, when she had pressed her way through the teeming crowd and touched the edge of Jesus's garment, the anointing flowed into her being, destroying every sickness and disease. She was instantly and verifiably healed.

> *"And straightway the fountain of her blood was dried up, and she felt in her body that she was healed of that plague. And Jesus, immediately knowing in himself that virtue had gone out of him, turned him about in*

*the press and said, who touched my clothes?" Mark 5:29-30*

But here is the point; Jesus knew immediately that the anointing had flowed from Him to heal her. And so he said, "Who touched me? Of course, many people must have been touching, considering He was amidst a huge crowd, but it was only her touch that caused "virtue" (the anointing) to flow towards her.

"How does this anointing flow through us?" You may ask. The answer lies in the Holy Spirit, the divine conduit through which the healing power flows and manifests. Like a river of living water, the Holy Spirit carries the anointing, infusing it into our very being, bringing about total soundness in our Spirit, soul, and physical body. Through our connection with the Holy Spirit, we also become vessels of healing and channels through which the anointing can freely flow to other people.

## TRANSMISSION BY THE SPOKEN WORD

The anointing can be transmitted from vessel to vessel. It can flow from one person to another. Like electricity, the anointing can be transmitted through 3 different mediums. The first is via the spoken word. The second is via physical contact, and the third is through other materials. Time will fail me to go deeper into these methods of transmission., But for the sake of this book, I will focus on the medium of the spoken word.

Like any other anointing, the healing anointing flows with the word. The Holy Spirit always goes in the direction of the spoken word. Of course, the first assignment of the word in healing is to build faith. But it is also a means to transmit healing power—the anointing. The Bible says, *"He sent his word, healed them, and delivered them from their destructions."* Psalm 107:20

Wherever the word goes, the anointing flows. The spoken word is one major way to transmit the healing anointing. That's what happens when it combines with the gift of word of knowledge or word of wisdom. As you release that word, healing manifests. It is the same when you command healing by faith. As you speak it forth, the anointing latches on it, and as people respond in faith, they experience the corresponding manifestation of whatever was spoken.

## THE PLACE OF FAITH

The next very important factor in the flow of the anointing is faith. Our faith acts as an electric conductor, allowing the healing anointing to flow freely into our lives. Just as a small spark can ignite a roaring fire, a flicker of faith can activate the power of the anointing, bringing about miraculous healing and restoration. Where there is faith, the healing anointing will flow and heal the sick. But where faith is lacking, the anointing will NOT flow, no matter how much you pray.

Like electricity, the voltage is inversely proportional

to resistance. If resistance goes down, voyage goes up; voltage goes down if resistance goes up. It is like that with unbelief. It acts as resistance or an insulator to the flow of God's power. That is why faith is a very important factor in the anointing flow. When Jesus went to His hometown, he could not heal the sick or perform significant miracles. In other words, He tried to minister to some people, but it didn't work. "Is that even possible?" You may ask. Of course, yes!

> *"And he went out from thence and came into his own country...And he could there do no mighty work, save that he laid his hands upon a few sick folks and healed them. And he marveled because of their unbelief."*
> Mark 6:1, 5-6

Of course, He had the anointing on him; but He could not transmit it to them. Their collective unbelief vehemently resisted the flow of the anointing on His life. How sad! They knew Him too much in the flesh to believe any miracle could happen through Him. He was the carpenter's son, remember? Some even called Him "the carpenter."

Rather than having faith in their healing and miracles, they were offended. And the result was that Jesus could not do significant miracles in their midst. Their unbelief short-circuited the flow of God's anointing towards them. The lesson is that nothing works without faith. Like the woman we discussed earlier, her faith made the difference.

Another good example is in the book of Acts, where Paul taught in the city of Lystra: A man in Lystra was lame from birth. As Paul proceeded with his teaching, he suddenly discerned that this lame man had faith to be healed. So, he pulled him up (Acts 14:8-10). Indeed, faith is very critical to the flow of the healing anointing. Once faith is in place, the anointing will be transmitted wherever needed.

## HEALING THE BROKENHEARTED

It is important to emphasize the healing of broken hearts. The most powerful aspect of the anointing is its ability to bring healing and restoration to every area of our lives. God not only heals bodies, but he also heals hearts. Jesus talked about healing the brokenhearted.

*"The Spirit of the Lord is upon me because he hath anointed me to preach the gospel to the poor; he hath sent me to heal the brokenhearted..." Luke 4:18*

The truth is, no matter how healthy you are in your body, you are sick if you are not whole in your soul. Many medical doctors have confirmed that most sicknesses result directly from emotional issues. More diseases emanate from emotionally related issues than from others. When people go through an unpleasant emotional experience, they are more likely to develop illness, unlike when they are emotionally sound.

The state of your mind and emotions largely influence

your health. That is why the Bible talks about prospering as your soul prospers (3 John 2). But the good news is that the anointing can handle all infirmities, no matter what. Not only does the anointing address physical ailments, but it also heals emotional wounds and mends broken hearts. Just as a loving touch brings comfort and reassurance, the anointing's gentle presence brings solace to our troubled souls. It embraces us in times of sorrow, releasing the burden of pain and replacing it with a profound sense of peace and joy. The anointing binds the brokenhearted, mending the shattered pieces and restoring emotional well-being.

The healing anointing is a bridge that connects the physical, emotional, and spiritual realms of existence. Through the anointing, we are healed and empowered to bring healing to others. It is a call to action, an invitation to become vessels of compassion and agents of transformation. As you allow the healing anointing to flow through you, you become an ambassador of hope, carrying the torch of healing to a world in need.

# 6

## THE PRICE FOR THE ANOINTING

# CHAPTER SIX

# THE PRICE FOR THE ANOINTING

T he anointing is not something we can earn or achieve through our efforts, but it is a gift freely given to those seeking it. Certain factors must be in place to receive and walk in the anointing. Although the anointing is available to every believer through the baptism of the Holy Spirit, not every believer gets to operate in its fullness, because it comes with a cost. Operating in the fullness of the anointing carries a huge spiritual cost. Being filled with the Spirit is one thing; experiencing the fullness of God's power is another thing altogether.

At the baptism of the Holy Spirit, the believer is

introduced into God's school of spiritual power (the river of living water). Still, by paying the required price, he is launched into a higher dimension of God's power (represented by the rain of the Spirit.) The truth is, the anointing will cost you everything. You cannot want everything without giving up everything; it just doesn't work that way. Remember, the secret to enjoying all of God is all of you.

The costs of the anointing are spiritual disciplines required to unlock the floodgates of God's power through our lives. These spiritual disciplines enable us to align ourselves with God's purposes, deepen our intimacy with Him and position ourselves to receive His supernatural empowerment. Our focus in this chapter is on the significance of spiritual hunger, consecration, prayer, fasting, and sacrifice in pursuing the fullness of the Spirit. Ultimately, we will examine the impact of a spirit-filled life on the anointing. The anointing of the Holy Spirit is God's dynamic power made available. But to experience the manifestations of that power, we must pay the price.

## 1. The price of spiritual hunger.

The first and most important step or price in the journey to the anointing is a desperate hunger for it—spiritual hunger. If you want the anointing on your life, you must be hungry! Nobody can experience the depths of God's anointing without a desperate hunger. Recognizing that the anointing is not attained through casual or lukewarm pursuit is crucial. There comes a time when the desire to experience more of God's power becomes a burning passion.

Spiritual hunger is an insatiable desire for the presence of God, His power, and His purposes. It is the recognition that there is more to be experienced in our relationship with Him. Just as physical hunger drives us to seek nourishment, spiritual hunger compels us to seek a deeper experience with God. When we desire and hunger for the anointing, we make ourselves candidates to receive it.

Jesus declared, "Blessed are they which do hunger and thirst after righteousness: for they shall be filled." Matthew 5:6

Spiritual hunger is a major key to accessing the supernatural. Notice: it says, "They which DO HUNGER AND THIRST..." That means they are perpetually hungry for more of God. They are not hungry one minute and then lack hunger the next minute. Instead, they DO HUNGER. That life of perpetual hunger is depicted in scripture with the deer. Hunger is the typical life of the deer.

> *"As the hart panteth after the water brooks, so panteth my soul after thee, O God. My soul thirsteth for God, for the living God: when shall I come and appear before God?" Psalm 42:1-2*

85

The deer is always hunting for more water. It has an insatiable desire for water. We can say the deer is perpetually thirsty and NEVER satisfied. As a result, it is always seeking an oasis to drink from. It is this hunger that keeps it seeking after water. In the same way, our spiritual hunger drives us to seek and pursue God and his power.

Spiritual hunger is not a passive longing but an active pursuit of God. It involves seeking Him wholeheartedly, desiring His presence, and longing for His anointing. King David, a man after God's own heart, expressed his spiritual hunger in Psalms:

> *"O God, thou art my God; early will I seek thee: my soul thirsteth for thee, my flesh longeth for thee in a dry and thirsty land, where no water is; To see thy power and thy glory, so as I have seen thee in the sanctuary. Because thy lovingkindness is better than life, my lips shall praise thee." Psalm 63:1-3*

David's hunger for God propelled him to experience the anointing in his life. David was both a priest, King, and prophet. And the beautiful thing was that he was anointed for all three offices, as we saw earlier in this book. The powerful thing about hunger and thirst for God is the promise of satisfaction. The scriptures assure us that those who hunger after righteousness shall be satisfied. Whether it is a hunger for more of God, a deeper walk with Him, or a hunger for the anointing, there is a promise of satisfaction. Through Isaiah the prophet, God extends an invitation to the thirsty and the hungry, promising to satisfy their needs abundantly. Here's what it says:

> *"Ho, every one that thirsteth, come ye to the waters, and he that hath no money; come ye, buy, and eat; yea, come, buy wine and milk without money and without price. Wherefore do ye spend money for that which is not bread? And your labor for that which satisfieth not? hearken diligently unto me, and eat ye that which is good, and let your soul delight itself in fatness."*
> *Isaiah 55:1-3*

That is an open call to the spiritually hungry to be satisfied. In the scripture above, wine and milk are metaphors for spiritual realities, which could mean the anointing or any other spiritual treasure, as it were. And then it says to buy and eat.... without money. If someone is to buy something, it means that the item is not free. There is a cost to it. And if one is to buy it without money, another currency is required. Money is not the only currency in existence. There are other currencies with higher purchasing power than any currency. And when it comes to spiritual things, money is not the currency. And like the above scripture strongly suggests, hunger is the currency required. Hunger is the currency for purchasing the anointing.

## 1. Start with awareness.

But it all begins with awareness. To become anointed, you need to gain adequate knowledge of the anointing. Hunger is stirred up by knowledge. Nobody ever desires nor pursues anything they are completely oblivious about. Awareness is what is required to wet your appetite spiritually. Physically speaking, it is like walking by a restaurant or a bakery. As soon as you perceive the aroma of freshly baked bread or delicious dishes, your appetite becomes aroused, leading to hunger. Sometimes, you feel like stopping by to get a loaf of bread. That is just how it is with spiritual things like the anointing.

Unfortunately, many believers remain unaware of the potential and power of the anointing available to them. As a result, they lack the hunger required to pursue it. As we study the scripture, we discover accounts of many individuals who were anointed by God and the impact it had on their lives and ministries. These examples serve as an invitation to hunger for the same anointing in our lives. This deep longing in our soul drives us to go the extra mile in pursuing higher dimensions of the anointing. The proof of desire is pursuit. If you are not reaching for it, you are not hungry enough. In the secret place of communion with Him, we are transformed into men and women of spiritual might.

The anointing is not reserved for a select few; it is available to all who hunger. Spiritual hunger is the key that unlocks the door to experiencing the anointing in our lives. As we cultivate a desperate hunger for God and seek intimacy, we position ourselves to receive and walk in the anointing. Amazingly, the Lord honors those who earnestly seek Him with all their hearts. "And ye shall seek me, and find me when ye shall search for me with all your heart." Jeremiah 29:13

## 2. The price of consecration.

Consecration is a major prerequisite to operate in the anointing. You cannot carry anointing in one hand and sin in the other. It is like carrying petrol and fire in both hands. If you do, you will learn a very bitter lesson in your lifetime. Sin will bring corruption to the anointing and disrepute to God's name. Nothing pollutes the anointing like a life of sin. Here is what Solomon had to say about sin and the anointing.

> *"Dead flies cause the ointment of the apothecary to send forth a stinking savor: so doth a little folly him that is in reputation for wisdom and honor." Ecclesiastes 10:1*

The author of Ecclesiastes likened sin to "dead flies" inside the ointment. And that is what sin does to the anointing. One of the most consistent and paramount characteristics of God is His holiness. God is pure and will not fraternize with anyone whose ways contradict His.

> *"Thou art of purer eyes than to behold evil, and canst not look on iniquity: wherefore lookest thou upon them that deal treacherously, and holdest thy tongue when the wicked devoureth the man that is more righteous than he?" Habakkuk 1:13*

But with consecration comes powers and God's glory in your life. That is the relevance of consecration in the pursuit of the anointing.

To be consecrated means to separate from sin, Satan, and the world unto God. When something is consecrated to God, it belongs to God and ceases to be used for any common purpose. It involves surrendering oneself wholly to God, including every aspect of life, to His lordship. It requires a heart fully yielded and willing to obey God's commands. To be truly consecrated, we must lay aside worldly desires, selfish ambitions, and sinful habits and open the door for the anointing to flow freely into our lives. Consecration makes holy, and holiness is essential for experiencing God's power. Holiness involves avoiding sin, embracing righteousness, and living by God's standards.

As we yield to the Holy Spirit's work in our lives and let Him sanctify our hearts, we become conformed to Christ's image; and empowered by the Holy Spirit. That is one of the most critical prices required for the anointing. Consecrate your life to God and prepare for a huge outpouring of God's Spirit.

## 3. The price of prayer.

Prayer is a vital key to experiencing God's power in our lives. Through prayer, we communicate with God, expressing our desires, seeking His guidance, and aligning our hearts with His will. Prayer opens the door for God to work in and through us, allowing His power to flow into every area of our lives. In the place of prayer, we cultivate intimacy with God, and as we spend quality time in His presence, listening to His voice, and growing in our relationship with Him, we make way for the anointing.

It is in the place of prayer that our faith is strengthened, our burdens are lifted, and our Spirit is refreshed. As we pour out our hearts in prayer, God equips us with His dynamic power and enables us to walk in His purposes. It takes earnestness in prayer to make God's power available.

*"Confess your faults one to another, and pray one for another, that ye may be healed. The effectual fervent prayer of a righteous man availeth much."* (James 5:16). To understand what Bible means by the phrase, "availeth much," let's read the same scripture from the Amplified version:

*"...The earnest (heartfelt, continued) prayer of a righteous man makes tremendous power available [dynamic in its working]."*

It is through fervent prayer that we make tremendous power available. The more you spend time praying, the more you operate in the anointing. In other words, you won't get anointed just because you casually recited the Lord's Prayer. If you experience God's power like never before, you will have to subscribe to a life of prayer—an earnest (heartfelt, continued) prayer.

## 4. The price of fasting.

Fasting is another essential step in experiencing and walking in God's power. It involves willingly abstaining from food or other activities for a specific period, seeking God's presence, and devoting ourselves to prayer. It is a spiritual discipline that helps break the power of the flesh and draws believers closer to God. Fasting is a powerful spiritual discipline that humbles us, heightens our spiritual sensitivity, and helps us break through thick spiritual barriers that seek to stop us.

The powerful thing about fasting is its capacity to shift our focus from earthly cravings to a deeper hunger for God. It helps us detach from worldly distractions and tune our hearts to hear God more clearly. Fasting also serves as a spiritual weapon against the forces of darkness, strengthening our spiritual authority and enabling us to overcome spiritual battles. In the school of spiritual power, fasting is a must. When Paul talked about some of the sacrifices he had to make in pursuing his assignment, he mentioned fasting as something he did very often.

*"In weariness and painfulness, in watchings often, in hunger and thirst, in fastings often, in cold and nakedness." 2 Corinthians 11:27*

Jesus also emphasized and demonstrated the importance of fasting in life and ministry. It was after Jesus went into the wilderness for forty days, fasting, praying, and overcoming temptation, that the power of God on him was provoked. The Bible speaks of how he returned in the power of the Spirit (the anointing):

*"And Jesus returned in the power of the Spirit into Galilee: and there went out a fame of him through all the region round about." Luke 4:14*

Fasting is closely associated with prayer. It is prayer that gives fasting its value. If you are fasting but not praying, it means you have completely missed the point. After Jesus ascended into heaven, His disciples had to tarry in Jerusalem untill they are endued with power (Luke 24:49). Tarring may have necessitated fasting as they wait for the promise of the Holy Spirit. That is not a coincidence, but instead a testament to the relevance of fasting and prayer to the anointing. As they prayed, the Holy Spirit came upon them like cloven tongues of fire. They were divinely empowered to bear true witness to the resurrection of Christ. Combining prayer and fasting creates a powerful atmosphere for releasing the anointing.

## 5. The price of sacrifice.

Another powerful price to pay for the anointing is sacrifice. Activating the anointing requires a willingness to sacrifice for God and His kingdom. Registering your commitment to any course is through the things you are willing to give up for its sake. To understand sacrifice, think about what Jesus did on the cross of Calvary. Jesus laid aside His glory in heaven and came to earth to die a shameful death on Calvary's cross. Sacrifice involves giving up something of value for the sake of God's kingdom. It may involve giving up personal desires, time, resources, or comfort to pursue kingdom advancements. Sacrifice demonstrates a heart that is fully committed to God and His purposes. Through sacrificial living, believers position themselves to receive and walk in the fullness of God's power. There is so much more to say about sacrifice, but for want of space, we would move on to something else very important.

### Practice a spirit-filled life.

To walk constantly in the anointing of the Holy Spirit, you need to master the dynamics of the spirit-filled life. Maintaining a spirit-filled life is very vital to operating in the anointing. When we allow ourselves to be filled with the Holy Spirit, we open the floodgates to the anointing. We become conduits of God's love and mercy, instruments through which the miraculous can occur. It is not our strength or ability that brings about these supernatural realities but rather our surrender to the divine flow of God's Spirit.

As a believer, you can only receive the baptism of the Holy Spirit once; like what we find in Acts 2:4, but you will constantly need to be "refilled" with the Spirit to remain spiritually buoyant and in the right position to discharge your daily responsibilities. If you have studied the apostles, you will discover they were constantly refilled with the Spirit. Every time they prayed and communed with God, they were filled afresh with the Spirit.

> *"And when they had prayed, the place was shaken where they were assembled together; and they were all filled with the Holy Spirit, and they spake the word of God with boldness." Acts 4:31*

If you don't understand this, you will think they just got baptized in the Holy Spirit again. But we know they were already baptized in the Holy Spirit in chapter two (2) of the Acts. So, this is not about Holy Spirit baptism but about remaining Spirit-filled. In the book of Ephesians, the Bible talks about being filled with the Spirit:

> *"And be not drunk with wine, wherein is excess; but be filled with the Spirit; Speaking to yourselves in psalms and hymns and spiritual songs, singing and making*

*melody in your heart to the Lord; Giving thanks always for all things unto God and the Father in the name of our Lord Jesus Christ." Ephesians 5:18-20*

The phrase "be filled" is rendered as "be being filed" in the original test, which refers to a state of "continuous infilling" with the Holy Spirit. Continuous infilling is something ongoing. As you pray, you are filled again and again with a fresh anointing. That was what David prophesied about when he declared, "But my horn shalt thou exalt like the horn of a unicorn: I shall be anointed with fresh oil." Psalm 92:10

This passage isn't focusing on the oil's freshness but rather on the renewal of anointing. David spoke of being anointed anew with oil, which symbolizes this spiritual anointing. Much like contemporary believers, David anticipated frequent anointings. Truly, living a life filled with the Spirit is essential for maintaining a consistent flow of anointing. Moreover, cultivating an intimate relationship with the Holy Spirit positions us to receive and radiate the anointing, facilitating healing and restoration for ourselves and others.

When Jesus was present on earth, His anointing was demonstrated through the miracles He performed and the lives He transformed. Jesus bore the anointing within Him and operated in its fullness. As a result, demons, diseases, and malevolent forces could not resist the power emanating from Him. Nevertheless, anointing is not simply a spectacle of power. It's the outcome of a deep, intimate connection with the Lord. We access the anointing by embracing spiritual hunger, consecration, prayer, fasting, and sacrifice, making it readily available to fulfill all needs.

# 7

## GO FOR THE ANOINTING

# CHAPTER SEVEN

# GO FOR THE ANOINTING

All the treasures of heaven are encapsulated in the person and power of the Holy Spirit. Nothing in the world surpasses the treasure of having the presence and power of the Holy Spirit at work in your life. When God gave us Jesus, He gave us everything; when He gave us the Holy Spirit, He gave us Himself. And with the Holy Spirit comes dynamic power to cause remarkable changes in every area of human endeavor.

To have the anointing is to have power, and to lack the anointing is to be bankrupt of power. What will you do without power? How far can you go without the tangible manifestation of God's omnipotent ability in your life? And with a broken and hurting world before us, we have no option but to pursue God's power like never before.

After the resurrection of Jesus, He instructed his disciples to preach the gospel to every nation of the earth. That instruction is typically referred to as the great commission:

> *"And Jesus came and spake unto them, saying, All power is given unto me in heaven and in earth. Go ye therefore, and teach all nations, baptizing them in the name of the Father, and of the Son, and the Holy Spirit: Teaching them to observe all things whatsoever I have commanded you: and, lo, I am with you always, even unto the end of the world." Matthew 28:18-20*

But without the anointing of the Holy Spirit, they could not have executed such a huge commission. Jesus, knowing the place of the anointing, further instructed them to tarry until they were endued with God's Power. By that, He was referring to the coming of the Holy Spirit on them.

> *"And, behold, I send the promise of my Father upon you: but tarry ye in the city of Jerusalem, until ye be endued with power from on high." Luke 24:49*

Jesus left them with the great commission and the

promise of the Father—a promise to send them the Holy Spirit. And as they all obeyed and waited patiently for God's promises, they were filled with God's Spirit. The Holy Spirit mantled on them with such power and glory that they could do extraordinary things in God's name.

## Anointing makes the difference.

The anointing of the Holy Spirit is what makes all the difference. Once someone is anointed, that anointing transforms a person from a coward and weakling into a person of boldness, courage, and extraordinary power.

It was the anointing that made the difference for all the disciples of Jesus. Having watched their master taken away and shamefully crucified, they were somewhat petrified and overwhelmed. What could be more demoralizing? Imagine having your hope for a better future completely dashed almost overnight! It was a painful experience and season for them until the very day the Holy Spirit came down to empower them. At that moment, fear was exchanged with courage and boldness; ordinary was replaced with extraordinary, and the natural quickly gave way to the supernatural. Judging by how Peter responded to the crowd attracted to their Holy "chaos," this was evident. At the instance of the Holy Spirit, they were all baptized and spoke in strange tongues.

*"And suddenly there came a sound from heaven as*

*of a rushing mighty wind, and it filled all the house where they were sitting. And there appeared unto them cloven tongues like as of fire, and it sat upon each of them. And they were all filled with the Holy Spirit, and began to speak with other tongues, as the Spirit gave them utterance." Acts 2:2-4*

That attracted the attention of thousands of passersby. Strangely enough, these teeming visitors heard the disciples speak their native languages, including those who had traveled to Jerusalem from distant lands as far as Asia, Europe, America, Africa, and the like.

*"And there were dwelling at Jerusalem Jews, devout men, out of every nation under heaven. Now when this was noised abroad, the multitude came together and was confounded because every man heard them speak in his own language. And they were all amazed and marveled, saying one to another, Behold, are not all these which speak Galilaeans? And how hear we every man in our own tongue, wherein we were born? Parthians, Medes, and Elamites, and the dwellers in Mesopotamia, and in Judaea, and Cappadocia, Pontus, Asia, Phrygia, and Pamphylia, in Egypt, and in the parts of Libya about Cyrene, and strangers of Rome, Jews, and proselytes..." Acts 2:5-10*

And when Peter would respond to their "doubts" concerning what was going on, he spoke with unquestionable audacity. Anyone who knows about the fishermen of that day would tell you that it was rather abnormal for Peter to speak out with such audacity. How could an ordinary fisherman speak with such compelling power that over 3,000 people surrendered to the gospel of Christ? Imagine standing before a large crowd of probably over four thousand people to convince them about one newfound faith. And to think that you were able to persuade 3,000 of them to get saved is something that calls for deep reflection. I am talking about people who have never heard anything about the gospel. It could only have been due to a supernatural power operating through Peter.

In another unrelated event, as we see in the book of Acts, we are told that they took notice of the boldness of Peter and John:

> *"Now when they saw the boldness of Peter and John, and perceived that they were unlearned and ignorant men, they marveled, and they took knowledge of them, that they had been with Jesus." Acts 4:13*

What made the difference? It was because of the Holy Spirit's power working through them. Of course, we are told the disciples' newfound boldness was because He had been with Jesus. But we also know that the power of the Holy Spirit had imparted them with such boldness. The same Peter who could not withstand a little girl's threat on the night of Jesus' arrest could now speak with boldness and power. Isn't it amazing how the anointing could transform people's lives?

Through the power of the Holy Spirit, Peter healed the sick, raised the dead, cast out the devil, and did many mighty miracles. By the anointing of the Holy Spirit manifesting tangibly through him, the lame man at the beautiful gate leaped and walked (Acts 3:8-9). All the mighty deeds recorded in the Book of Acts came to be by the power of the Holy Spirit. Hallelujah!

The anointing gives us the courage to step out in faith and pursue our dreams. It enables us to overcome our fears and doubts and take bold steps toward the future that God has for us. We have seen many examples of individuals who were anointed for great things. A great example is David. David was anointed to be the king of Israel. However, he was only a shepherd boy at the time. But David went on to defeat the giant named Goliath, thereby liberating Israel's army from the reproach of Goliath all because of the anointing. Ultimately, he became one of the greatest kings in Israel's history.

Likewise, the apostle Paul was anointed to preach the gospel to the Gentiles. He faced many challenges and obstacles along the way, but because he was anointed, he persevered and made an impact that is still palpable today.

But the anointing is not just for the "greats" of the Bible. It is for all believers of today, no matter who they are or their circumstances. Whether in Bible days or our present day, everyone who has ever made a significant difference in the kingdom of God did so via the anointing.

What about Jesus Christ Himself? The anointing made a huge difference in the earthly life and ministry of Jesus. Although He was fully God and fully man, His humanity on earth demands that He is imparted with the anointing as man would.

> *"How God anointed Jesus of Nazareth with the Holy Spirit and with power, who went about doing good and healing all who were oppressed by the devil, for God was with Him." (Acts 10:38)*

After this, there was a sudden miraculous outbreak as He became like a moving and talking atomic bomb. Everywhere He went, He did extraordinary things! He healed every sickness and disease, raised the dead, and destroyed all works of darkness in people's lives. He was practically in command of the supernatural. He was in command of extraordinary results! Untill He returned in the power of the Holy Spirit (Luke 4:14), many considered Jesus as a carpenter's son.

What does that tell us? The anointing is what makes the difference:

- The anointing turns you into another man.
- The anointing puts you in command of extraordinary results (exploits).

- The anointing transforms you into a sign and a wonder.

- The anointing unlocks in you the supernatural life.

- Life without the anointing is a complete waste of time

Do not attempt to accomplish anything for God except with the anointing. Don't preach, teach, pastor, prophesy, or administer without the anointing. A one-time foremost revivalist would say, "In all thy getting, get the anointing" And may I add, "No matter what else you lack, make sure you don't lack the anointing." As someone who represents the Almighty God, you must strive to carry the tangible manifestation of God's power in your life and ministry. God's finger and mark of dignity must be visible in your life to command the attention of the world around you.

## ANOINTING BY IMPARTATION

A vital element of this subject of the anointing is how to receive it. There are two principles of scriptural ways by which anyone can receive the anointing. The first is through a direct encounter with God. God can show up and put His anointing on you. The second method of receiving the anointing is by impartation—from a person already anointed with the anointing you desire. This is very critical. Having shared many valuable things with you through this book, I realize that if I didn't share this with you, I would have done you a great disservice. The anointing can be imparted. If truth be told, all graces, all anointing, and all spiritual gifts can be imparted by the vessels that have them.

> *"For I long to see you, that I may impart unto you some spiritual gift, to the end ye may be established."*
> Romans 1:11

## IT'S RIGHT THERE

Now let me share a very vital secret of impartation with you: The anointing of every ministry is found in two places, first the messenger; and, secondly, the message itself. That is so profound! If you understand this, consider yourself blessed:

**1. The messenger (carrying the message).**

In other words, if you want the anointing operational in any ministry, go for the minister himself. A good Biblical example of direct impartation was between Elijah and Elisha. Elisha was a protégée of Elijah, and by consistently serving and honoring Elijah, he eventually received a double of his anointing. A good example in our day is pastor Benny Hinn, who was imparted directly by Katherine Kulman of blessed memory.

Anointing flows like an ocean, as it were, from a region of higher concentration to a region of lower concentration. It flows from those who have it to those who lack it. And so, if you position yourself rightly, it will flow to you.

In the parable of the ten virgins (Matthew 25), we read that when the foolish virgins went to ask for oil from the wise virgins, they were advised to go to those who sell oil to buy for themselves.

> *"lamps. And the foolish said unto the wise, Give us of your oil; for our lamps are gone out. But the wise answered, saying, Not so; lest there be not enough for us and you: but go ye rather to them that sell, and buy for yourselves." Matthew 25:8-10*

That is not to say that the anointing can be bought; of course not! It is just letting us know it comes at a cost. But here's the point: If you want the anointing, go to God or those who already have it and get it from them. And impartation is the way you receive it from them.

If you can find the carrier of such graces or anointing and connect appropriately, you will contact the same anointing they embody. That is why it always seems like those serving certain men of God become copies of them. They talk, preach, pray, and sometimes dress like them. It is not an attempt to destroy people's originality; it is only the practical operation of the law of impartation.

Another way you can be imparted apart from serving the anointing like Elisha is through partnering financially with that person. I am not discussing partnering with the ministry persé but with the person. There is a difference between giving to a man of God and giving to his ministry. They are NOT the same. One will assist the man; the other will assist with the work. When you give generously to a man of God, when you partner with him, you become a partaker of his grace (Philippians 1:7). For this reason, Paul prayed passionately for the Thessalonian church (Philippians 4:19).

## 2. The message itself.

The second place to contact the anointing in any ministry is through messages. If you want the anointing in a ministry, go after the materials (recorded messages or written (documentation). Many people today and in the past have contacted strange orders of anointing from God's choicest servants by simply listening to their tapes or reading their books. This is so powerful because even after the persons carrying the anointing are gone, we can still access and receive the anointing they carried through their materials. In other words, you can receive the anointing on anyone you desire their anointing, using this method of impartation. I tell you what, if you do, you will never be the same again!

## THE POSSIBILITIES ARE TRULY ENDLESS

The anointing can give us the strength and courage to overcome our challenges and achieve things that we never thought possible. If you are stuck or unsure of your purpose or how your life will turn out, ask God to anoint you. Ask Him to give you the courage to step out in faith and pursue the dreams and goals He has placed in your heart. Ask Him to reveal in you the possibilities that are available to you through His anointing.

With the anointing, anything is possible. No dream is too big; no challenge is too great. When we are anointed, we are empowered to do all things through Christ, who strengthens us (Philippians 4:13). If we are adequately anointed, we can scale any wall before us.

Are you ready to embrace the possibilities that are available through the anointing? Are you ready to bear authentic witness to Christ's resurrection? Are you intersected and passionate about becoming proof producers in your generation? Then go for the anointing. We all are assured that it will be ours if we pay the price! Oh, hallelujah! Hallelujah!! As you receive the anointing and deploy it to meet needs, answer questions and solve generational problems, always be reminded that with God's anointing on your life, the possibilities are truly endless.

# About the Author

Bishop Andrew Pusey has studied and successfully ranked in credentials to ordained bishop with the Church of God International. He is a prophet and evangelist to the nations.

His ministry has seen diverse manifestations of the Holy Spirit's power and grace. He is a spirit filled christian for over 30 years. He is a sought-after speaker for ministry ,church conferences and revivals.

His ministry has documented miracles, healing, deliverance, and breakthroughs in people's lives. He is married to Mrs. Odetta Alves-Pusey, and they reside in New York.